Embracing Special-Needs Families

A Church Model for Ministering to Families of Children and Adults with Disabilities

Handbook from Stonebriar Community Church
Additional material from Insight for Living

INSIGHT *for* LIVING

U. S. 1-800-772-8888
Canada 1-800-663-7639
Australia 1800 772 888
www.insight.org

Embracing Special-Needs Families
A Church Model for Ministering to Families
of Children and Adults with Disabilities

Contributing writers:

Kelly Arabie	Bryce Klabunde	Graham Lyons
Colleen Swindoll Dane	Michelle Kopfer	Robert A. Pyne, Th.D.
Suzanne Keffer	Sue Lindahl	Cliff Ritter

ISBN: 1-57972-524-4
Cover design: Shawn Sturm
Cover photos: (Top photo) Chuck Swindoll and Jonathan Dane; (Middle photo): The Dane Family (left to right) Colleen, Ashley, Jonathan, Mark, and Austin; (Bottom photo): Sue Lindahl and Jonathan Dane.

Contents

Introduction

Special Needs Ministry Handbook, Stonebriar Community Church

Insight for Living Articles

For Families of Children with Special Needs

Contents *(Insight for Living Articles . . . Continued)*

INSIGHT *for* LIVING

Committed to Excellence in Communicating Biblical Truth and Its Application

A Word from Insight for Living

Dear Friend,

In His parable of the great banquet, Jesus reminds us that the kingdom of God welcomes all who will come. The invitation to the Master's table specifically goes out to people with disabilities. "Bring in the poor, the crippled, the blind and the lame" (Luke 14:21 NIV).

Pastor Chuck Swindoll and the leaders at Stonebriar Community Church have developed exciting methods to carry on Christ's invitation to people with disabilities and their families. It's a privilege to link arms with the church to help other pastors and leaders start their own special needs ministries.

In this resource, you will find an introductory article describing ways you can launch your special needs ministry based on the model of the special needs ministry at Stonebriar Community Church. In the second section, you'll find the Special Needs Handbook from SCC. It is available for you to use as a source of ideas, and we invite you to adapt it to your own situation. The final section includes articles from the pastoral ministries department at Insight for Living. This section will give you some biblical principles and personal testimonies on which you can build your ministry of encouragement.

Thank you for your interest in making room at your church's table for people with disabilities and families of children with special needs!

Partnering for the kingdom,

Bryce A. Klabunde
Vice President of Pastoral Ministries
Insight for Living

Dear Friend,

Since the inception of Stonebriar Community Church, its leadership has placed importance on ministering to all of God's loved ones. This includes children and adults who have disabilities. People who are blind, deaf, developmentally delayed, or medically fragile all need to feel loved and accepted. We know that reaching out to those with special needs visually embraces the Gospel in action.

Our ministry began with only a few children, but as we have grown we have maintained our philosophy of serving "one child/adult at a time." Joni Eareckson Tada, founder of Joni and Friends, says, "Disability ministry is an outreach to a minority with great implications for the majority."

This handbook is a practical "hands-on" guide to serving those with special needs. It has been developed to instruct and guide volunteers at Stonebriar. Much of it comes from practical experience and from the wisdom of Spirit-led ministry.

I trust that it will be helpful to those with a heart for special needs ministry, giving you a clear framework for developing your own ministry program.

Sincerely,

Sue Lindahl

Sue Lindahl
Special Needs Coordinator
Stonebriar Community Church
Frisco, Texas

You Can Start a Special Needs Ministry!

A Look at One Church's Example as a Model for Your Ministry

by Bryce Klabunde

Vice President, Pastoral Ministries, Insight for Living

Bright, festive decorations adorn the walls and dangle from the ceiling. A plump green bean bag sits next to low tables. Large wooden puzzles wait for little hands. A "sling" swing hangs from a doorway that leads to a second room, where a climbing tube and two giant cushioned wedges anticipate playtime. Colorful letters spell out "FunZone!"

These two Sunday school rooms at Stonebriar Community Church in Frisco, Texas, are the fruit of a vision to build a nurturing place adapted to the special needs of children with disabilities.

For parents of children with special needs, these rooms represent an open-arms welcome for their family. Many families in their situation simply don't attend church because there is no suitable place to bring their children on Sundays. A small but growing number of churches are beginning to see the outreach potential of forming a Special Needs Ministry.

Perhaps you would like to build such a ministry program at your church. Where do you begin? Here are a few ideas to get you started based on the Special Needs Ministry of Stonebriar Community Church.

Begin with a Biblical Mandate

Special Needs Ministries grow out of the ministry model of Jesus, who reached out to individuals who were lame, blind, deaf, and diseased (see Matthew 9:35–38). By healing people's physical infirmities, He demonstrated His ability to heal our greater spiritual disease. Special Needs Ministries follow the Savior's example, demonstrating the love of Christ to individuals with disabilities and inviting all people to respond to His gospel.

Craft a Mission

A mission is a declaration of purpose that gives direction to those involved in the ministry. Why does this ministry exist? What principles does it promote? What makes it unique from other programs in the church?

The heart of the Special Needs Ministry at Stonebriar Community Church is a desire for people affected by disabilities and their families to come to a personal relationship with Jesus Christ. Along with that desire are several basic principles about special needs ministry that you can use to guide your mission priorities.

Ministry Model

- Children with disabilities should have the opportunity to grow in their Christian faith through a nurturing environment adapted to their special needs.

- When ready and able, children with disabilities should be included in the regular Sunday school program. This philosophy of inclusion teaches the children in the church about the love of Christ for those who are affected with disabilities.

- People with disabilities should be enabled to share their gifts with the church body through service, leadership, and worship.

- The facilities of the church building should accommodate and welcome people with disabilities.

- Families of children with disabilities should find a support network in the church through group interaction, counseling, and respite opportunities.

Recruit People with a Heart for Children with Special Needs

Often special needs ministries begin with one individual feeling a burden to reach out to people with disabilities. Sandra Burns was that person at Stonebriar Community Church. In 1998, when the church was founded, she recruited others to help care for five children with special needs during the church services.

From that small beginning, the ministry grew, and in 2001, the church hired Sue Lindahl part-time to oversee thirty volunteers, an assistant coordinator, and an interpreter for the deaf.

How can you raise interest in this ministry? Ask your pastor to feature your plans in the church newsletter and announce a meeting in your Sunday morning worship folder for people interested in helping. You may wish to publish a church survey in the Sunday morning worship folder to measure the level of need and interest. Then make personal invitations to those who respond. A phone call to a friend is often the most effective method of recruiting.

Use Quality Special Needs Ministry Materials

Many denominations provide manuals for churches that wish to begin disability ministries. Check with your denominational regional headquarters to find out what is available.

Sue Lindahl and her staff at Stonebriar Community Church used the materials provided by Joni and Friends, the disability outreach of Joni Eareckson Tada, and have found them to be very helpful in getting started. The manual is titled *How to Create an Effective Disabilities Outreach in Your Church* and can be obtained through this unique ministry. You can order a manual by calling (818) 707-5664. Or you can contact them via the Internet at www.joniandfriends.org. Ministry representatives in various major cities in the United States are available to assist you in setting up your program.

Develop Training Materials, Policies, and Forms

Ministering to children with special needs requires specific training. The manual from Joni and Friends includes information and handout sheets on the following topics that you can use in your training:

1. Understanding the World of Disability

2. A Model of Inclusion

3. Overcoming Barriers

Other training materials, sample policies, and forms are included in the Stonebriar Community Church Special Needs Ministry Handbook that is included in this book.

Launch the Programs

With the foundation laid, you can build various programs to minister to families with special needs. Here are a few of the programs that Stonebriar Community Church offers families of children with special needs.

Facilities. The church building meets and exceeds the standards of the American Disabilities Act (ADA) that requires handicapped parking, ramps, doorways, and bathrooms. The children's playground is ADA approved as well. In addition, there are parking spaces for families of children with special needs.

Equipment. Wheelchairs are available upon request and large print Bibles are available for the visually impaired. The sound system is designed to assist the hearing impaired as well.

Special Needs Sunday School. Two special needs classrooms are equipped to accommodate children with disabilities. The rooms are staffed with trained volunteers to keep children during the first and second services.

Inclusion Buddy System. For children with disabilities who can participate in the regular Sunday school classes, there are trained "buddies" available to accompany them. The buddies help the children participate in the classroom activities and feel included.

Deaf Ministry. Interpretation for the deaf is available during the first service in the worship center.

Respite Ministry with Nursing Care. Families of children with special needs who are members of the church can bring their children to the church on the second Saturday of every month. The special needs classrooms are available and staffed with volunteers and a nurse to keep the children while the parents enjoy an evening out. Parents who leave their children must complete an extensive medical release form that is notarized and kept on file.

Support Group. An Early Childhood Intervention support group meets twice a month. Parents can discuss their concerns and receive helpful information.

Ministry Model

Prayer Ministry. A group of concerned individuals gathers every other week to pray for the families with special-needs children and for the ministry.

Special Olympics Field Day. Each summer, families come to the church for a day of sporting events and fun for children with special needs.

Conclusion

During His ministry, Jesus often shined the spotlight of compassion on people with disabilities. As you develop special needs programs in your church, you carry on this important aspect of His ministry. May the Lord bless you in your ministry effort.

Special Needs Ministry Handbook

www.stonebriar.org

S T O N E B R I A R   C O M M U N I T Y   C H U R C H

Vision

One of the major aspects of the Lord Jesus Christ's ministry on earth was His outreach to children and to people who had disabilities. He repeatedly invited individuals who were blind, deaf, lame, and diseased to enter the kingdom of God through the gift of salvation. Jesus also worked mightily in the lives of disabled people by healing them.

In Jesus' day, people with disabilities had a very important role in God's work on earth. They were at the forefront of much of what happened in the Gospels. Through these people, God showed His great love and compassion. We are to follow our Lord's footsteps in reaching out to children and adults who have disabilities.

Goals

- To **understand** and implement the biblical principles of disability ministry.

- To **hold** to the philosophy of ministry, which is one of "inclusiveness."

- To intentionally and systematically **evangelize** and disciple people with disabilities.

- To **integrate** people with disabilities into the life of the church body, giving them the opportunity to have active roles in serving God.

- To **support** the families of the disabled through providing counseling, if necessary.

- To **provide** Special Needs Ministry staff who have a heart for ministry to the disabled.

- To **establish** the Special Needs Ministry to serve as a witness to the community for meeting the needs of disabled persons spiritually, physically, and socially.

Core Values

Character
in Ourselves

– Living a life characterized
by integrity as a result of
a growing relationship
with Jesus Christ.

Honor
to Others

– Providing an atmosphere of respect
where each person can contribute and thrive.

Grace in Our
Relationships

– Practicing thoughtfulness, kindness, generosity, courtesy, freedom, forgiveness,
encouragement, and appreciation of others' differences.

Excellence
in Our Pursuits

– Producing the highest quality ministry program,
materials, and personal service possible.

Glory
to Our God

– Living by faith by
entrusting our talents,
finances, and plans to
God's control.

Accountability
to One Another

– Willingness to answer for one's life, characterized by
vulnerability, teachability, honesty, and availability.

S T O N E B R I A R   C O M M U N I T Y   C H U R C H

Special Needs Ministry Events

Sunday School Classes

- *9:00 A.M. and 10:45 A.M. services*

- *Inclusion* (Buddy provided)

- *Separate classrooms*—Room 148 and Room 150

    - If a visitor drops off a child with special-needs into any classroom other than 148 or 150, the teacher should welcome the child, then contact the Special Needs Coordinator, Sue Lindahl, at Extension 5270. Sue will come and observe the child in the classroom.

    - If a parent desires that their special needs child be included only in the special needs classroom, please direct them to Room 148.

Early Childhood Intervention (ECI)

- *First and third Mondays*, 10:30 A.M.–12 noon. Room 148.

FunZone (Respite Ministry)

- *Second Saturday of every month*, 6:00 P.M.–10:00 P.M.

- *Nurse on-site* for medically fragile children.

- *For reservations to attend FunZone* or if you need to cancel your reservation, contact Tammy Cameron by the Thursday before *FunZone*.

Deaf Ministry

- *9:00 A.M. service*—Interpreter available.

Ladies' Night Out

- *For mothers of special-needs children and women volunteers.*

Men's Night Out

- *For fathers of special-needs children and male volunteers.*

Special Needs Safety Policies and Procedures

- A minimum of **two adults** should be present in every room at all times, except in the event of an emergency.

- **Classroom doors** should have clear glass windows that allow easy view of the classroom activities without interrupting the teaching process. Doors without glass should remain open.

- **Youth buddies** will be at least 13 years old to serve with children 2 years old and older. Childcare providers serving in the nursery (birth to age 2) will be 16 years of age or older. *Youth buddies should never care for children alone.*

- **Security badges** will be worn by all childcare providers identifying them as authorized by Stonebriar Community Church.

- **Children** entering the classroom will have been signed in by their parent(s) and have an ID badge. Since we have medically fragile children in Room 148/150, only children with special needs are allowed in the classroom.

- Children will be **released** only to a parent who has the corresponding ID numbers. No child is to be released to another child or sibling under the age of 16.

- **Medications**—Special needs buddies are not to give or apply any medications. If a child needs medication, the parent must administer it.

Restroom Guidelines

- **Preschool:** When a preschooler needs assistance, an adult may enter the cubicle and a second adult must be in visual contact. Only women should assist girls and boys in the restroom. The outside restroom door must remain propped open.

- **Elementary children:** When a child is taking longer than seems necessary, calling the child by name from the door is appropriate. Unless a child requires assistance, special needs buddies should not be alone with the child. Teen buddies should not escort the children to the restroom unless accompanied by an adult.

Classroom Evacuation

- Acquaint yourself with the evacuation route for your classroom. It is posted near the exit door of your classroom.

- Acquaint yourself with the alternate evacuation route for adjoining classrooms, should your primary exit be blocked.

- Before evacuation, count the number of Special Needs Ministry participants in your class. If you have an attendance sheet with names, take it with you.

S T O N E B R I A R   C O M M U N I T Y   C H U R C H

Church Office Injury Report

Name: _____ Age: _____ Sex: ☐ M ☐ F

Address: _____ City:_____ State:_____ Zip:_____

Name of parent(s):_____Phone: _____

Date and time of accident: _____

Describe in detail how the child was injured, including location, names, and actions

of all children and adults involved:_____

_____

_____

_____

Describe the child's injuries and what action was taken to treat the injuries: _____

_____

How and when were the parents notified?_____

_____

Please list the names and phone numbers of witnesses to accident: _____

_____

_____

_____

Additional comments:_____

_____

Your name, address, and phone number: _____

_____

Special Needs Emergency Procedures

- Immediately notify the Special Needs Coordinator, who is in radio contact with the on-site medical support team and who will call 911 as needed and the Pastor of Children's Ministries.

- Please pull the child's medical chart and medical release form located on the counter in Room 148.

- Use the security ID system to contact parents. Parents of medically fragile children will carry pagers.

- An accident form must be completed by the special needs buddy in the classroom and turned into the Children's Ministries office as soon as possible.

Personal-Safety Boundaries

Physical touch can be essential in the nurturing process, characteristic of our ministry with children. Childcare providers need to be sensitive to the special needs of each child. Physical contact should be age-appropriate.

Guidelines for appropriate touch:

- Meet the child at eye level.

- Hold the child's hand while listening or speaking to him/her or when walking to an activity.

- Put your arm around the shoulder of a child when comforting or quieting is needed.

- Pat a child's head, hand, shoulder, or back when encouraging.

- Gently hold the shoulder or chin of a child when redirecting behavior.

The following types of touch must be avoided:

- Kissing or coaxing a child to kiss you.

- Extended hugging and tickling.

- Touching a child in any area that is normally covered by a bathing suit.

- Carrying an older child or sitting him/her on your lap.

- Being alone with a child.

- Giving a full contact, body-to-body hug.

- Piggy-back rides/"horsey" rides.

Points to Remember When You Meet a Person Who Has a Disability

Joni and Friends–Family Retreats • Adapted from The National Easter Seal Society
Used with permission

- Remember that a person who has a disability is a *person*—like anyone else.

- Relax. If you don't know what to do or say, allow the person who has a disability to help put *you* at ease.

- Explore your mutual interests in a friendly way. The person likely has many interests besides those connected with the disability.

- Offer assistance *if asked* or if the need seems obvious, but don't overdo it or insist on it. Respect the person's right to indicate the kind of help he/she needs or wants.

- Talk about the disability if it comes up naturally, without prying. Be guided by the wishes of the person with the disability.

- Appreciate what the person can do. The difficulties the person may be facing may stem more from society's attitudes and barriers than from the disability itself.

- Be considerate of the extra time it might take for a person with a disability to get things said or done. For example, let the person set the pace in walking or talking.

- Remember that we all have handicaps; it's just that on some of us they don't show.

- Speak directly to a person who has a disability. Don't consider a companion to be a conversational go-between.

- Don't move a wheelchair or crutches out of reach of a person who uses them.

- Never start to push a wheelchair without first asking the occupant if you may do so.

- When pushing a wheelchair up or down steps, ramps, curbs, or other obstructions, ask the person how he/she wants you to proceed.

- Don't lean on a person's wheelchair when talking.

- Give whole, unhurried attention to the person who has difficulty speaking. Don't talk for the person, but give help when needed. Keep your manner encouraging rather than correcting. When necessary, ask questions that require short answers or a nod or shake of the head.

- Speak calmly, slowly, and distinctly to a person who has a hearing problem or some other difficulty understanding. Stand in front of the person and use gestures to aid communication. When full understanding is doubtful, write notes.

Behavior Challenges

While children need and deserve clear boundaries, discipline at church is unique. It's unlike what happens at home or at school. It's done by a person that the child may only see one hour a week and in an unfamiliar classroom. Teachers who talk about love and kindness must also communicate rules and administer consequences, all in a 90-minute session. So, what should discipline at church look like?

- *Discipline is training that corrects, molds, or perfects.*

- *Discipline is an ongoing process.*

- *Discipline leads to self-discipline as the child grows older.*

- *Discipline is rooted in love.*

Preventing Problems
- *Set clear limits or boundaries.*
    - It is never acceptable to hurt anyone.
    - It is never acceptable to damage anything.

- *Let the children know that you are their buddy during class.*
    - Speak in a low, pleasant, but firm voice. Never use sarcasm.
    - Treat each child with dignity and respect.
    - Catch a child being good! Focus on positive reinforcement.

- *Never forget the value of each child.* The child who is the hardest to love needs it most.

- *Allow the children to make choices*, giving them responsibility for their actions. Be sure that children understand the choice to obey or disobey established rules is theirs, but if they choose to disobey, they are also choosing the consequences of the disobedience.

- *Redirect the child's attention.*

- *Remain in control.* NEVER TOUCH A CHILD IN ANGER OR ADMINISTER PHYSICAL PUNISHMENT OF ANY KIND. Say the child's name and try to maintain eye contact. If necessary, gently place your hands on the child's shoulders to keep his or her attention.

- *Enforce prearranged consequences.*

    - A preschool child may have "time out" or "thinking time." The chair should be placed at some distance from the group, but never in a corner or outside the room. Time out should never last longer than one minute per age of the child.

    - Elementary age children may have the three-count system. #1—give a warning. #2—restate the rule and inform them of the consequence. #3—escort the child to the Special Needs Coordinator, who may recommend a meeting with the Pastor of Children's Ministries and the child's parent(s). Maintain consistency! If the same child goes through this procedure a second time, the parents may be asked to accompany the child if he/she is to return to the class.

Ten Steps to Changing Diapers

1. Collect all necessary supplies (gloves, plastic bag, wipes, etc.)

2. Wash hands and put on gloves.

3. Talk with child about what you are doing.

4. Place child on clean, disposable surface (wax paper). Never turn away from child while he/she is on the changing table.

5. Remove the wet or soiled diaper. Place in plastic bag.

6. Use wipes, wiping front to back. Place all wipes in plastic bag with soiled diaper.

7. Put clean diaper on child and remove child from changing area.

8. Remove disposable paper cover from changing table. Place disposable paper in plastic bag. Spray changing area thoroughly with bleach solution, wiping with paper towel.

9. Place paper towel, gloves, and any other used items into plastic bag, tie knot, and throw it all away.

10. Wash hands thoroughly.

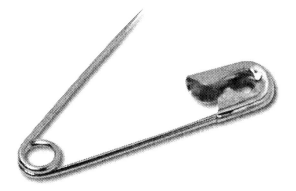

Buddies Procedures

General Procedures:

- No children or adults on tables or chairs, please.

- All teachers and volunteers should sign in on classroom rosters.

- All toys and supplies should be neatly put away after use.

- Throw away all trash and empty cups into the garbage cans.

- Clean and clear the counters.

- Push in chairs neatly under tables; please do not stack the chairs.

- Make sure snack container lids are closed tightly and put away.

- Use sweeper on floor where needed.

- Flush toilets if needed.

- Turn off the bathroom and classroom lights.

- Return visitor security badges to the Badge Booth on your way out of the building.

Specific Procedures for Room 148:

- If a new family comes to visit, have them fill out the two yellow forms located on the counter.

- No unauthorized parents/teachers may use rooms 148 or 150 as a shortcut to the other hallway.

- Wash hands when you are volunteering. Use gloves when you are changing diapers.

- Follow classroom schedule posted by the telephone. (If the classroom telephone rings, please answer it.)

Thank you for keeping His House in great condition!

Avoiding Inclusion Confusion

A Few Tips for a Disability-Friendly Program from Joni and Friends
Used with permission

Physical Disabilities

- If children are physically unable to create a craft or participate in an activity, allow them to borrow your hands . . . but don't forget to let them use their imagination. Make them active participants by encouraging them to direct your actions. Ask questions such as, "Should we make a bird or an elephant?" "Big ears or little ears?" "A tail or not a tail?" "What color is the bird?"

- Provide larger toys, crayons, utensils, or dolls for children who have difficulty grasping items.

- Some children will have an easier time painting or coloring if the paper is taped to the table surface. Others may be more successful (and have more fun!) at toe painting than finger painting.

- When singing, tap the rhythm lightly on the child's hand or leg. Engage the children in lots of motions or sign language. Encourage kids to use jingle bells or drums, flags, scarves, or streamers for praise (especially for those with less fine motor control who may have difficulty with the motions).

- For children whose grasp is weak, bring strips of Velcro to fasten everything from a paintbrush to a rhythm instrument to a child's hand or wrist. This will help stabilize the object as the child holds it.

- Objects (craft supplies, etc.) can be placed on a Rubbermaid non-slip pad to hold them in place.

- During playtime, position children in a comfortable and safe way that will allow them to have maximum range of motion.

Blind and Visually Impaired

- Avoid using vague words when giving instruction, especially words associated with visual space ("The glue is over there"). Instead, use a familiar point of reference ("The glue is just above your paper by your right hand").

- Allow the child time to feel the props, stage, craft materials, or game pieces before beginning.

- Use sound cues, musical toys, and interesting textures or sounds to enhance the child's play experience.

- Use vivid, bright colors for children with limited visual ability. They can enjoy and respond to colors, even if they can't clearly see objects.

- If a child has some vision, place craft or lesson materials on larger sheet of black paper. This helps bring the other materials into focus.

- If a child is to color on paper, place craft paper on a larger piece of sandpaper. This will help the child know where the edges of the paper are.

- Describe the colors, lights, shapes, and sizes of the objects in the child's surroundings.

- During music, ask if you can gently guide the child's hands or arms to teach them the motions.

Deaf and Hearing Impaired

- Compensate for loss of hearing by making the most out of the senses of sight and touch. Use visual and physical examples as you explain directions.

- Remember body language and facial expressions are part of communication. Be animated so that what cannot be heard from your voice can be read in your posture and face. But, remember that over-exaggerating may actually make it more difficult to understand.

- As often as possible, get to the child's eye level so he/she can comfortably see your face when you speak.

- If the child is able, encourage him/her to communicate about his/her surroundings and experiences. Ask open-ended questions, such as, "Tell me about what you are making" or "What was your favorite part of the drama?"

Mental Disabilities

- Avoid long lists of instructions. Allow the child to finish one step before explaining the next.

- Repeat instructions frequently, using the same words and phrases.

- When necessary, gently turn the child's head to face you or the activity to help focus attention.

- Limit choices. Too many choices are confusing and distracting.

- Allow the child to make a simpler version of the craft. Keep rules less complicated for games and activities.

- Provide well-marked boundaries for physical activity.

- If you know or suspect that a child is capable of a task, don't do it for the child.

- Avoid seating child near distractions when possible (in high-traffic areas, near air conditioner, near loud children, etc.).

- Familiarize the child with the daily concept using concrete terms before visiting the drama room. Re-explain the daily concept following the drama, explaining any abstract examples.

Learning Disabilities and ADD/ADHD

- Break instructions into short segments. If necessary, give one instruction at a time.

- Get the child's attention before talking to him/her.

- Expect that you will need to repeat instructions. Stay calm and patient. Be a safe person from whom children may request help.

- As much as possible, maintain eye contact with the ones who have difficulties comprehending during verbal instructions.

- Whenever possible, demonstrate instructions visually. The more ways you give input, the easier it is for children to understand and remember.

- Limit choices. Too many options are confusing and distracting.

- Allow for movement during activities if possible (lie on the floor, sit with legs out or legs crossed, kneel, stand to do crafts, etc.).

- Provide reminders about time when necessary. Give 10-minute, 5-minute, and 1-minute warnings toward the end of an activity. Help the child start to wrap up a little early to aid in transitions.

Autistic and Sensory-Sensitive

- Eliminate as many nonessential distractions as possible. It may help some children to face a plain wall rather than sitting in the middle of the room or in the midst of a flurry of activity.

- Be aware of environmental factors to which the child is most sensitive (noises, lights, motion, personal space violations, etc.). Think through the program and be prepared to remove the child to a nearby, less stimulating spot before anxiety escalates.

- Keep "escape" toys handy that can be used in a repetitive way (objects that roll, spin, rock, etc.). These allow the child to tune out distractions that may be disturbing by concentrating on the toys.

- A headset to block out noises may calm some children at stressful times.

Special Needs Buddy Agreement

Feeling called by God, I agree to the following guidelines as a buddy at _____
_____(church) for the period of_____ to _____ .

With God's help, I will:
*   Serve in Children's Ministries during 1st hour/2nd hour in Room _____and/or *FunZone.*

As a buddy, I am committed to our Lord:
*   I have a personal relationship with Jesus Christ that I desire to model for children.
*   I enjoy studying God's Word regularly and desire to grow in my faith and commitment to Him (through personal study, adult classes, or home Bible study groups).

Our church:
*   I worship regularly with our church family.
*   I support the core values and leadership of _____ (church).

My student(s):
*   I enjoy children and desire for them to know of God's love and concern for their lives.
*   I will keep any medical history of the child confidential.
*   I will care for my students individually through prayer.
*   I will be faithful in attendance, arriving at least 15 minutes before the session begins.
*   If I must be absent, I will contact a fellow team member to substitute and alert the Special Needs Coordinator.
*   I will stay until the parent picks up the child.
*   I will help as much as is necessary in any activity. If the child doesn't need assistance, I will stand back and monitor. I am there for the child, not as an aide to the classroom teacher. My goal is for the child to function independently in the classroom.
*   I will care for the cleanup of my classroom, returning all items to the proper place, and pushing chairs to the table.

My teaching team:
*   I will participate in training events during the year.
*   I will express my needs as a buddy to the Special Needs Coordinator.
*   All activities outside the regularly scheduled Special Needs Ministry classes/events **must be pre-approved by the Special Needs Coordinator.**

Name:_____ Date: _____
Please sign and return.

S T O N E B R I A R   C O M M U N I T Y   C H U R C H

Special Needs Ministry
Permission/Authorization Agreement

Please read the following statements carefully and initial in the designated space indicating that you have read, understand, and agree to the provisions.

_____ I have fully disclosed to_____(church) all pertinent facts and medical conditions about my child(ren)'s special needs and accept full responsibility for failure to do so.

_____ I understand that no medication will be given.

_____ In case of an emergency or accident, I understand that the Frisco EMS (911) will be called. I authorize EMS to administer any medical treatment, medication, or appliance deemed necessary by EMS. I also authorize transportation by EMS to the nearest appropriate medical facility,as determined by EMS. I understand that I will be responsible for payment of all EMS, hospital, and/or physician charges for emergency services to my child.

I have read and initiated the above permission/authorization statements and agree to the terms designated in each.

Signed:_____ Date:_____
(Parent or Legal Guardian)

Signed:_____ Date:_____
(Parent or Legal Guardian)

S T O N E B R I A R   C O M M U N I T Y   C H U R C H

Sunday School Special Needs Assessment

Date:_____ Student's name:_____ Birth date:_____

Parents' names:_____

Parents' address:_____City:_____ State:_____ Zip:_____

Parents' e-mail:_____ Phone (Home):_____ (Cell):_____

Siblings *(names and ages)*: _____

School student attends:_____Grade:_____

Specific type of disability: _____

  1. Diagnosis:_____

  2. Description in lay terms: _____

Is your child on medication? ☐ Yes ☐ No Type(s):_____

Seizures:_____Allergies: _____

Foods/drinks we should not give your child:_____

Assistance needed with eating/drinking:_____

Is help needed for personal hygiene?_____

Communication skills:_____

Reading level:_____Writing level:_____

What are your child's strengths?_____

Weaknesses: _____

Older children–gifts/talents he/she would like to use in the classroom: _____

Child's understanding of God/relationship with Christ:_____

Past Sunday school/church experience:_____

Activities child enjoys most: _____

Special fears: _____

Describe your child's behavior, if adverse. What do you do to control this behavior?

_____

Any additional information we should be aware of:_____

_____

_____

S T O N E B R I A R   C O M M U N I T Y   C H U R C H

Reminders for Volunteers

- Plan to be at church from 5:30 P.M. to 10:30 P.M. on Saturday nights.

- Sign in on Volunteer Log. (Fill out an application/security check if you have not already done so.)

- Dinner will be provided.

- Wear comfortable clothes; aprons will be provided.

- Store personal items in Room 148 closet.

- No dangle earrings, bracelets, necklaces, heavy perfume, or hairspray.

- Do not smoke immediately before or during *FunZone*.

- Check children's diapers frequently. Use gloves to change diapers.

- Go in pairs to the bathroom.

- Wash hands often and before contact with a different child.

- Perform NO medical procedures.

- Do not feed children your food (they may have allergies).

- Do not lean on a person's wheelchair when talking.

- Do not work at *FunZone* if you or anyone in your family has a contagious disease.

- If there is a discipline issue, tell the person in charge.

- Toys should not be shared among children who are medically fragile.

- Do not walk on floor mats.

- Clean rooms and put things back in proper order for Sunday school.

- Have fun with the children.

- Emergency procedures:
  - In case of a life-threatening emergency, the person in charge will call 911.
  - Seizures can be a common problem for children with medical conditions. Seizures lasting more than five minutes constitute an emergency.

Schedule

5:00 – 5:15 P.M.	Arrival of person in charge
5:15 – 5:30 P.M.	Remainder of volunteers arrive
5:30 – 5:50 P.M.	Volunteers eat dinner and meet for family overview (Room 130)
5:50 – 6:00 P.M.	Be available to help parents as they arrive
6:00 – 6:15 P.M.	Families arrive
6:15 – 7:15 P.M.	Children wash hands and eat dinner. (They bring their own.) Those who have already eaten may either go to the playground or have free play in the big room with supervision.
7:15 – 7:30 P.M.	Water/bathroom break
7:30 – 8:30 P.M.	Stations or special event (puppets, music, bounce house, fire truck, policeman)

- LEGO™ corner
- Puzzle corner
- Crafts
- Coloring
- Blocks
- Trains/race cars
- Board games
- Foose Ball

8:30 – 8:45 P.M.	Snack time
8:45 – 9:45 P.M.	Movie (Children may choose free play or listen to storyteller.)
9:45 – 10:00 P.M.	Clean up/prepare to go home
10:00 – 10:15 P.M.	Quick group meeting
10:15 – 10:30 P.M.	Volunteers put everything away in closets (Room 150)

S T O N E B R I A R   C O M M U N I T Y   C H U R C H

Application for Respite Services

I. Family Information

Date: _____

Father's name: _____ Birth date: _____

Address: _____ City: _____ State: _____ Zip: _____

Employer: _____

Phone (Home): _____ (Cell): _____ E-mail: _____

Mother's name: _____ Birth date: _____

Address (if different): _____ City: _____ State: _____ Zip: _____

Employer: _____

Phone (Home): _____ (Cell): _____ E-mail: _____

Parents' anniversary: _____

Child(ren) requiring medical or special supervision:

_____ Gender: ☐ M ☐ F Age: ____ Birth date: _____

_____ Gender: ☐ M ☐ F Age: ____ Birth date: _____

_____ Gender: ☐ M ☐ F Age: ____ Birth date: _____

Siblings:

_____ Gender: ☐ M ☐ F Age: ____ Birth date: _____

_____ Gender: ☐ M ☐ F Age: ____ Birth date: _____

_____ Gender: ☐ M ☐ F Age: ____ Birth date: _____

Other family members living at home and ages: _____

_____

Child's primary diagnosis: _____

Primary physician: _____ Physician's phone: _____

Physician's address: ____ _____ City: _____ State: _____ Zip: _____

31

II. Emergency Contacts (Other than doctor)

In case of an emergency, the following persons may be called and are authorized to pick up my child:

(At least one contact must be provided. Positive identification must be provided before your child will be released.)

Name:_____ Phone:_____ Cell:_____

Address:_____ City:_____ State:_____ Zip: _____

Driver's license:_____ Relationship:_____

Name:_____ Phone:_____ Cell:_____

Address:_____ City:_____ State:_____ Zip: _____

Driver's license:_____ Relationship:_____

III. Permission/Authorization Agreement

Please read the following statements carefully and initial in the designated space indicating that you have read, understand, and agree to the provisions.

_____ I have fully disclosed to Stonebriar Community Church all pertinent facts about my child(ren)'s special needs and accept full responsibility for failure to do so.

_____ If my child is enrolled in the Saturday night respite program, I authorize the staff to provide any required special treatments or procedures to my child while in respite care. I will provide written instructions and all necessary supplies and equipment for these procedures.

_____ I will supply all necessary food, drinks, snacks, and diapers/wipes for my child(ren).

_____ In case of an emergency or accident, I understand that the Frisco/Plano EMS (911) will be called. I authorize EMS to administer any medical treatment, medication, or appliance deemed necessary by EMS. I also authorize transportation by EMS to the nearest appropriate medical facility, as determined by EMS. I understand that I will be responsible for payment of all EMS, hospital, and physician charges for emergency services to my child.

I have read and initialed the above permission/authorization statements and agree to the terms designated in each:

Signed: _____ Date: _____
                  (Parent or Legal Guardian)

IV. Publicity Release

We encourage you to participate in our effort to help other families learn about the *FunZone*.

I ☐ **do** ☐ **do not** give permission for_____ to be photographed for use in press releases, journal articles, or other positive publicity related to *FunZone* and/or Stonebriar Community Church.

V. FunZone

I ☐ **do** ☐ **do not** give permission for my name, address, and phone number to be published in a Parent Directory for *FunZone*.

Signed: _____ Date: _____

(Parent or Legal Guardian)

S T O N E B R I A R   C O M M U N I T Y   C H U R C H

Special Needs Behavior Questionnaire
Your frankness will help our volunteers provide better care for your child(ren).

Name:_____ Gender: ☐ M ☐ F Birth date: _____ Current date: _____

1. Please describe your child's behavior problem (hits, runs away, throws objects, self abuse, etc.)_____

_____

_____

_____

2. What happens prior to/causes this behavior? Is it usually in response to something else?_____

_____

_____

_____

3. How often does this behavior occur?_____

_____

_____

_____

4. In what settings is this behavior likely to occur? (home, school, work, with strangers, etc.)_____

_____

_____

_____

5. What is the most successful way to deal with this behavior?_____

_____

_____

_____

6. Can you suggest a positive reinforcer for your child (items or experiences he/she especially enjoys)?_____

_____

_____

_____

_____

Special Needs Care Plan

We appreciate the opportunity to care for your children. Please complete the following information completely so that our non-medical and medical volunteers will know how best to care for your child(ren) and make their time with us comfortable, fun, and safe. Please complete one form for each special needs child who will be coming on Saturday nights.

NOTE: The attached hospital medical release form must be completed and NOTARIZED for each child in our care.

I. Family Information   Today's date:_____

Child's name:_____Gender: ☐ M ☐ F Birth date: _____

Parents/guardians: _____

II. Medical Information

Child's health needs (if applicable):_____

Medications taken on a regular basis:_____

_____

Immunizations: Is your child current on immunizations?   ☐ Yes ☐ No

If no, please explain:_____

Childhood diseases: Has your child had any of the childhood diseases (measles, chicken pox, mumps, etc.)? ☐ Yes ☐No   Dates and types:_____

Allergies: Does your child have any specific allergies to:

Drugs:_____

Food:_____

Insects/other:_____

Precautions (seizures, asthma, etc.):_____

_____

_____

_____   **Attach**

_____   **recent**

_____   **photo**

_____   **here**

_____

III. Care Needs

Vision: ☐ Normal   ☐ Impaired   ☐ Blind

Hearing: ☐ Normal   ☐ Impaired   ☐ Deaf   ☐ Hearing Aid

Motor: ☐ Head Control ☐ Rolls Over ☐ Sits   ☐ Crawls   ☐ Cruises
             ☐ Walks   ☐ Walker   ☐ Crutches   ☐ Braces   ☐ Wheelchair

Please describe any special positioning needs your child may have: _____

_____

Can communicate with others using:

☐ Speech ☐ Words ☐ Phrases ☐ Sentences ☐ Babbles ☐ Gestures
☐ Sign language   ☐ Other (Describe): _____

Language spoken at home: _____

Can Understand What Others Say: ☐ All of the time ☐ Most of the time
☐ Some of the time ☐ Recognizes voices of family members

Toileting Skills:
☐ Independent ☐ Currently being potty-trained ☐ Potty-trained, needs assistance
☐ Requires catheterization   **Diapers:** ☐ Cloth ☐ Disposables

How does your child indicate a need to use the toilet? _____

Indicate special toileting needs/schedule: _____

Eating Habits: ☐ Feeds self ☐ Requires feeding ☐ Bottle fed
Drinks from cup: ☐ By self   ☐ With assistance   ☐ Uses spoon   ☐ Uses fork
Eating schedule: _____
Special diet: _____ _____
Please describe any special assistance or adaptive utensils required for eating:

_____

Sleeping Habits:

At respite, my child can be placed in:

☐ Playpen ☐ Crib ☐ Floor mat   ☐ Other: _____

My child will be most comfortable placed on:

☐ Back   ☐ Side ☐ Stomach   ☐ Other: _____

Usual bed time: _____ Special routines: _____

III. Care Needs *(Continued)*

Behavior: (Check all that apply)

☐ Shy ☐ Outgoing ☐ Plays alone   ☐ Plays in groups

☐ Adapts to new situations well   ☐ Adapts to new situations with difficulty

☐ Responds to correction well   ☐ Responds to correction with difficulty

☐ Sometimes destructive   ☐ Sometimes threatens others

☐ Sometimes hits, bites, or hurts self/others ☐ Sometimes runs away

☐ Hyperactive and/or ADD

My child responds to separation from his/her parents by:_____

My child is best comforted by:_____

My child lets me know what he/she wants/needs by:_____

Play activities my child enjoys and/or participates in:_____

Permission has been granted to duplicate the following forms:

Church Office Injury Report

Special Needs Buddy Agreement

Special Needs Ministry Permission/ Authorization Agreement

Sunday School Special Needs Assessment

Application for Respite Services

Special Needs Behavior Questionnaire

Special Needs Care Plan

Please obtain an Authorization for Emergency Medical Treatment from your local hospital.

Insight for Living Articles

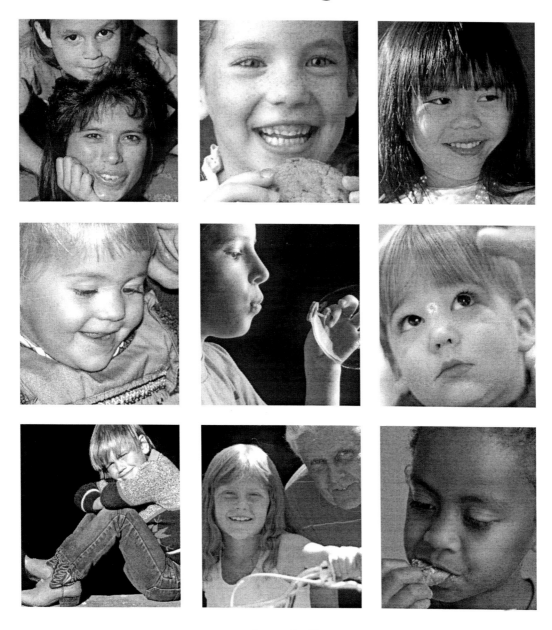

www.insight.org

A Dream Shattered, a Dream Renewed

Learning Your Baby Will Be Born with a Disability

by Michelle Kopfer

Women's Ministry Associate, Pastoral Ministries, Insight for Living

Leslie has just returned from the sterile obstetrics office, still in shock from the impact of the doctor's words to her and her husband. Their baby—their precious baby—is almost certain to be born with Down syndrome, bringing mental retardation, heart defects, and numerous other health problems. Leslie curls into a ball on her bed while her husband, Dan, still sits in the car, his head on the steering wheel. Tears can't release the pain that builds in their hearts over the devastating news. There may never be a high school graduation. Daddy may never walk his little girl down the aisle. Playgroups, family vacations—every one of Leslie's dreams has been shattered.

Leslie has a choice, according to Dr. Cole. She could make the choice to end the life of her child through an abortion or induced labor, or she could choose to live the life of a mother whose baby would never be like other children. Leslie's anguish, her uncertainty, and her fears for the future deluge her like a raging river in a stormy flood. How could she ever care for this child? How will they afford it? How will their family and friends respond? Why would the Lord allow her baby to be so ill? How could He possibly bring good from what seems like such a tragedy?

No words can comfort the sorrow parents in this situation must face, yet Scripture shines light on the choices they must make. God's Word can direct those steps, revealing clearly how our Lord views children who are born with disabilities.

God's View of a Special Baby

For you created my inmost being;
   you knit me together in my mother's womb.

I praise you because I am fearfully and wonderfully made;
   your works are wonderful,
   I know that full well.

My frame was not hidden from you
   when I was made in the secret place.

When I was woven together in the depths of the earth,
   your eyes saw my unformed body.

All the days ordained for me
   were written in your book
   before one of them came to be. (Psalm 139:13–16 NIV)

For Families of Children with Special Needs

These words describe every baby ever conceived—Leslie's baby, your baby. God's truth from this psalm tells us much about His work in the universe. He has intricately created each cell, each muscle, and every tissue in your baby. The Master Artisan wonderfully forms your baby no less wonderfully than He formed you. And yet our fallen world affects each of our bodies in many ways. Our differing levels of intelligence, struggles with disease, and the inevitable process of aging all remind us that our bodies and minds are not all they were originally created to be.

Despite these things, God's Word breathes truth and hope into our lives. The Craftsman who redeems also magnificently designed each of us. In this life we can experience redemption spiritually; and one day we will experience it physically when we join Him in heaven (see Philippians 3:20–21). Even still, the Author of Life maintains sole authority over your baby's life. We cannot usurp His authority. Our Creator places much value on your child. Learning of your child's disability is frightening, but you can step out in trust, because God's hand intricately shaped your child. He holds your baby's life in His loving hands.

God's Encouragement for You

> But now, this is what the Lord says—
> he who created you, O Jacob,
> he who formed you, O Israel:
> "Fear not, for I have redeemed you;
> I have summoned you by name; you are mine.
> When you pass through the waters,
> I will be with you;
> And when you pass through the rivers,
> they will not sweep over you.
> When you walk through the fire,
> you will not be burned;
> the flames will not set you ablaze.
> For I am the Lord, your God,
> the Holy One of Israel, your Savior." (Isaiah 43:1–3a NIV)

The Lord promises that He is with us. Just as He reassured His people Israel while their world was falling apart, so He reassures you. He created you and He is with you. If you walk along this valley, be at peace that your heavenly Father guards you from the flood. He is with you in the fire, keeping you safe. He will enable you to come through.

God's Strange Ways of Working

> But God chose the foolish things of the world to shame the wise; God chose the weak things of the world to shame the strong. He chose the lowly things of this world and the despised things—and the things that are not—to nullify the things that are, so that no one may boast before him. (1 Corinthians 1:27–29 NIV)

There is a strange economy in God's plan. At times, those who have the least of what the world considers valuable—autonomy, strength, intelligence—are the ones whom God most greatly gifts with what He values.

Consider Christ's praise of little children and their simple faith (see Matthew 18:1–6, Mark 10:13–16), and wonder in awe at the strange and special gifts God is giving to your child. Having different gifts may mean having greater gifts from God's point of view. As Paul pointed out, the weakest among us may, through their faith, shame the strong.

Though there is a time for sadness as you grieve lost hopes and dreams, there is a time also for rejoicing because you have been entrusted with a precious treasure. Just as Job was not chosen for his lack of faith but for his strength, so you have not been chosen for your weakness. Rather, the Lord has seen a great strength in you to bear the gift of this child. Not all gifts are of our own choosing; sometimes our only choice is how the gift is received. But we know we can trust the Giver, for He is good.

God's Exhortation to His People

Defend the cause of the weak and fatherless;
  maintain the rights of the poor and oppressed.

Rescue the weak and needy;
  deliver them from the hand of the wicked. (Psalm 82:3–4 NIV;
  see also Psalm 72:12–14)

Having a baby with a disability or disease may be one of the hardest things you will face. Yet as you trust the Author of Life, welcoming this child to our world for as long as He ordains, you defend the cause of the weak and the needy. You have rescued one of His own from death and chosen to trust our Father for the future. Be reassured, the Lord sees. He feels your pain; He sees your faithfulness. He will give you the strength you need to bear this burden and the joy you need to see His hand in the midst of it.

Preparing to Welcome Your Baby

1. Allow yourself time to develop new expectations and new dreams. You need time to mourn, releasing the dreams and hopes that you had and time to consider the new joys this child will bring to your life. Feeling sad as you let go of your first expectations does not mean you will not love your baby. It simply means taking time to develop new dreams and hopes.

2. Learn everything that you can about your child's illness. The more you know, the more prepared you will feel to handle this challenge. As you learn about your child's struggles in advance, you actually begin to build love in your heart for your special baby. Try library and Internet research, and ask your doctor for help.

3. Find out what resources your community offers. Many towns may have support for families struggling with the same challenges you will face. Some towns offer a night out for parents caring for disabled children. Others offer support groups. There are national groups for almost every area of disability; and these may be able to point you to helpful resources in your area.

4. Talk to other parents with children like yours. These relationships can be very helpful as new challenges arise, and you may discover that the joy these parents find in their child brings new encouragement to you. Ask your church, your doctor, and local advocacy groups for names of those who might be willing to talk about their experiences.

5. Ground yourself in the truth of God's Word. There will be moments of joy, but there will also be moments of sadness. Both are normal. Memorize verses that encourage you and make sure you spend regular time with the Lord in prayer and reading your Bible. Ask Him for joy and pray for your baby. The Lord who loves you completely is entrusting you with a fragile and precious life. He will provide for this gift He has given.

Weathering the Storm

Four Anchors for Parenting a Special-Needs Child

by Colleen Swindoll Dane

Special Needs Ministry Associate, Pastoral Ministries, Insight for Living

Ice blanketed the cars on that February dawn in 2000. I sat alone with my thoughts in a hospital just north of Dallas, Texas. The hospital had become a "second home" for our family, especially for our third child, Jonathan, and me.

Jonathan's birth gave us no indication of what was to come. Following a normal pregnancy and quick delivery, I never expected to travel down the painful path of countless hospital stays, tubes and needles, blood draws and breathing treatments. In his first year of life, Jonathan had fifteen ear infections, three bouts with a respiratory virus leaving scar tissue on his lungs, viruses that cleaned out his intestinal track, and fevers that soared to 105 degrees without warning.

With our first two children, Ashley and Austin, we struggled with the normal challenges of two young children born eighteen months apart. We battled acid reflux, colic, ear infections, allergies, and infant milk intolerance, but we made it through the sleepless nights and routine doctor appointments without much alarm. I didn't think I would make it through eleven days in February.

By that icy morning in February, Jonathan was fifteen months old, had his fifth bout with RSV (respiratory virus), Roto (intestinal) virus, allergies, severe asthma which required breathing treatments around the clock every three hours, and a systemic infection (blood illness sending disease throughout his entire body). For those eleven days, the doctors drew Jonathan's blood every day at 6 and 7 A.M. His IV sites were so infected we spent forty minutes trying to find a vein that would administer medication and fluid to attempt to keep his shell of a body alive. In addition, he was on eight separate medications needed to help him survive. I had no idea if Jonathan would make it through that day. The doctors and nurses prayed that things would turn around for our little guy.

Jonathan did make it. I thought we had seen the worst of it. Shortly after that stay, the immunologist said, "Mrs. Dane, your son will require the work of ten children. Are you ready for this?" How does one answer such a question when there is no option but to press on? I wondered where God was in all this. The best physicians we could contact only shook their heads in bewilderment at Jonathan's continually deteriorating condition. At times I pounded the air with my fists wondering where God was and why my pleas fell short of heaven's help.

Ashley's Question

Three months after that eleven-day stay in the hospital, Jonathan fell out of his

For Families of Children with Special Needs

crib and broke his left arm. As I rushed off to our "second home, Mark took Ashley and Austin to school. Silence spoke of the children's worries. Ashley, our seven-year-old daughter asked Mark, "Daddy, how come Jesus helps everybody else's family, but He doesn't help our family?"

How do you answer such a question from your child? Better yet, how do you answer the question for yourself . . . "Where are You, God? How come You seem to answer others' cries for help, and my cry goes on and on and on? You promise You will be there in times of need, yet my hope runs thin."

C. S. Lewis wrote shortly after the death of his wife, Joy, in the book *A Grief Observed*:

> When you are happy, so happy that you have no sense of needing Him . . . you will be—or so it feels—welcomed with open arms. But go to Him when your need is desperate, when all other help is vain, and what do you find? A door slammed in your face, and a sound of bolting and double bolting on the inside. After that, silence.[1]

Another book that has meant a great deal to me during this struggle has been *Making Sense out of Suffering*. In it, the author writes these very candid words:

> But the strongest case against God comes . . . from the billions of normal lives that are full of apparently pointless suffering. It is not just that the suffering is not deserved; it is that it seems random and pointless, distributed according to no rhyme or reason but mere chance, and working no good, no end. For every one who becomes a hero and a saint through suffering, there are ten who seem to become dehumanized, depressed, or despairing.[2]

A Lifelong Journey

The challenges did not end with the broken arm or the hospital stays. Shortly into his third year, Jonathan was diagnosed with Pervasive Development Disorder/Not otherwise specified (PDD, NOS), a category in the Autistic Spectrum Disorders. That's a fancy way for saying there is not a specific diagnosis, just a conglomeration of developmental delays, challenges, behaviors, and symptoms that we have yet to fully understand. By Christmas of 2001, we received the news that Jonathan would probably struggle with this for the rest of his life. In addition, by 2002 our oldest son, Austin, had been diagnosed with ADHD and language processing issues.

Five years ago Jonathan joined our family. The news that you have a child with lifelong special needs is a storm that can sink anyone's soul. It is an immense challenge that affects almost all areas of your life. But as one who is surviving, I have found four foundational truths that anchor the soul when the storms rage. Whether you have a special-needs child or you are beset with other afflictions, I encourage you to integrate these anchors into each moment of your day.

Anchor Yourself to His Word

The first anchor I secure myself to is the timeless, changeless, applicable Word of God. When mourning, I turn to the Psalms and read the Laments—the funeral songs—to find comfort and hope in Him. When alone, wondering where God is, I turn to the end of Genesis and read how God was with Joseph in the dark passages of his life. When seeking wisdom for practical living, I go to Proverbs and James. When weary, unable to plod on, I turn to Isaiah 40, Job 38–41, and Matthew 6 for reassurance that God will lift me when the burden is great. There is not a challenge in life where God is absent or unable to bring light to my dark path. So please, go to the first and most fundamental anchor in life, the Word of God. It restores hope and brings peace in the midst of storms.

Anchor Yourself in His Character

Second, in addition to the anchor of God's Word is the anchor knowing God's character. Only in Him do we find absolute strength, peace, joy, satisfaction, hope, trust, unconditional love, and so much more. When the raging winds blow, anchor yourself to the rock-solid character of God. He desires to be our strength in weak moments, our peace in the midst of pain, and our refuge in stormy seas. He will never leave us nor forsake us. In a fallen world, we will experience and endure countless hardships. Only in heaven will life be perfect, but He offers us an opportunity to cling to His perfect character in our imperfect world.

Anchor Yourself in His Sovereign Hand

Third, I have learned to place my trust in the unquestionable, sovereign hand of God. God is not partially sovereign. He is not in control only when we have it good and then out of the picture when it's tough. As Job stated to his struggling wife, "Shall we indeed accept good from God and not accept adversity?" (Job 2:10). How easy it is to shout from the rooftops that God is sovereign when we like our lives. But what about when we lose everything? Our long-standing faith is usually replaced with lingering doubt.

I do not know what the future holds for Jonathan or for others in my life that I hold so dear to my heart. But I do know that my faithful God is in complete control, and I accept the good and the tough as both being within His sovereign grasp. When life gets difficult, I am comforted by God's presence. When life brings blessing, I am comforted that God owns it all and I am only a caretaker of His property. It is all His. Letting go brings such freedom. The last anchor will show how letting go is possible.

Anchor Yourself to His Goodness

For the final anchor, I have found that meditating on the goodness of God closes the gap when my faith is failing. We are reminded in Hebrews 11 that faith is what we hope for but cannot see. There have been weeks and months when I did not see the evidence of my faith and when it appeared that God was not the least bit

For Families of Children with Special Needs

interested in my struggles. By meditating on the fact that God is a good God and desires good for my life, I held on.

You may ask, "What good can come from my circumstances? They're deplorable, and I find nothing good in this." It's true—bad things happen. Yet that is not the issue. The issue is how God transforms our weakness into His strength. In allowing Him to do so, you and I will watch God take the bad things of life and bring good things out of them. It will result in changing you as a mother or father. Perhaps there are selfishness issues, trust issues, areas of pride, selfish ambition, or self-seeking motives that surface in these difficult times. He will take what we are, burn out the bad, and purify our faith to be as pure gold. That is good! That is what happens as we walk the lonely roads of heartache and sorrow. I will never label heartache as good in itself. It's tough. But what comes from it is good, and that is what God takes delight in doing and seeing in every one of His children.

A Closing Prayer

By God's grace, we made it through those eleven days in February. Holding fast to those four anchors, we've made it through days far worse since that time. This is where I am in the journey. I'm not sure where you are. If you're on the journey, you know quick fixes don't exist. However, there is God. God supplies us with His inspired Word, His perfect character, His sovereign hand, and His incredible goodness. My prayer for you is that when the waves buffet your soul and when the winds rage against your hope, you, too, may find security in these four anchors.

---

1. C. S. Lewis, *A Grief Observed* (Boston, Mass.: Faber and Faber Limited, 1966), p. 7.
2. Peter Kreeft, *Making Sense Out of Suffering* (Ann Arbor, Mich.: Servant Books, 1986), p. 10.

Four Passages in the Lives of Parents with a Special-Needs Child

by Colleen Swindoll Dane
Special Needs Ministry Associate, Pastoral Ministries, Insight for Living

Not everything that is faced can be changed, but nothing can be changed until it is faced.   —*James Baldwin*

When one door of happiness closes, another one opens; but often we look so long at the closed door that we do not see the one which has opened for us.   —*Helen Keller*

* * *

I lay looking out the window from my bed in the maternity ward of a Minneapolis hospital on a Monday morning in the last week in March. The sky was leaden and the ground was covered with dirty snow. The dead, gray scene reflected my deep despair. Just the day before I had been told that my new-born son, Amar, my first child, most likely had Down syndrome. On Sunday I had felt numb disbelief. But today I knew that it was true. I see myself, as if in a movie, going home, carrying the baby. I walk up the steps and in through the front door, which closes behind me. And there the film stops. . . . Like a thwarted, hurt child saying, "I won't play" or "I won't eat," I thought, "I'll never practice law again"; "I'll never give another dinner party again." I thought, "I don't want to belong to the world of the retarded." . . .

Sooner or later we learn that determination, will power, household help, therapy, activities, parent groups, escapes, and all other outside support we may rely on aren't enough. Real staying power comes from trading activity for stillness. . . .

We come to a new place where we discover that we have been opened to love and transformed. We have new ways of seeing our creator, our child, our own humanity, and the rest of mankind. We have lived and learned the great human paradox that out of pain, sorrow, disappointment, and failure are forged growth, power, strength, and love.[1]

I sat quietly on January 1, 2003, reading the words of Barbara Gill, a fellow traveler in the world of disabilities. Like her, I was shaken to the core when I found out five years ago that my son Jonathan had a disability. Within the span of one day, my whole life changed.

53

For Families of Children with Special Needs

Throughout my journey, I discovered that my attempts to control life were often efforts to manage inner turmoil. I found that control is really an illusion, and coming face-to-face with special people who are challenged and disabled only illuminates that truth. Nonetheless, letting go of our attempts to control situations brings pain because we all long to have something to hold onto in this life. We want our expectations to be met; we want our longings to be attainable. We desire to have a little bit of heaven on earth.

But until we reach heaven, Jesus Christ's work in each of us is to loosen our grip on earthly things and tighten our hold on Him. No one can journey these quiet roads of transformation for you. It is on these paths—laden with disappointment and distress, anger and anguish—that Christ supplies strength, support, and comfort.

Many parents of children with disabilities feel like they're on a roller coaster. They feel the ups and downs, the accomplishments and failures, the joys and sorrows that seem to repeat themselves. At first, the world of disabilities appears to be a devastating closed door; over time, a window emerges and the light of hope appears.

Due to our experiences with our own disabled child, we see life through different eyes. We've come to learn that ordinary things are causes for celebration— a smile, eye contact, or movement of a finger or a toe. All of these are successes that we used to take for granted. We've seen that appreciating God's small blessings is a delightful way to live. But how do we move from sorrow to celebration? When our lives feel like a wild roller coaster ride, how do we move smoothly and successfully through it all?

In my experience of traveling in the special-needs world, I have identified four movements that occur on the roller coaster of life. These movements, or passages, do not take away the challenges, but they will help you to navigate the stormy waters without allowing your soul to sink into despair.

Movement One: From Expectations to Reality

In *Special Kids Need Special Parents*, Judith Loseff Lavin states, "Finding out that your child has special needs is an emotional earthquake. Everything seems broken, turned upside down. You stop trusting even the most mundane things. Life seems unsteady. You've been dealt a blow—a blow to your expectations."[2] All parents have expectations of what their children will look like, what they will become, what their interests will be, who they will marry, and so on. Whether we verbalize these expectations or not, our attitudes and actions are drawn from these deep wishing wells.

When our lives are drastically altered by a devastating diagnosis, our hopes and dreams die painful deaths. Healing comes when we move from the death of these dreams to the discovery that we can create new dreams, new hopes, and new joys that are defined by different parameters.

For Families of Children with Special Needs

When parents first receive a special-needs diagnosis, they may deny it, blame others, protest the diagnosis, or become extremely angry. These initial responses are a part of the grieving process, and they are healthy. But I have yet to meet a parent who desires to stay in the place of grief. That's unhealthy coping, and it's miserable! In order to move from the place of outrage, fear, protest, and blame, we must identify our expectations. Completing the phrases "I had hoped and dreamed . . . , I longed for . . . , I never imagined . . . , I always thought . . . " can help parents through this process.

When the imperfections of this world crash into our lives, we clutch for something to help us cope. The way to cope with pain this deep is to embrace the strength only Christ can provide. The perfect place is heaven, but we are not there yet. In order to live here, we need Christ's perfect nature, which provides strength for the weary and hope for the hurting. By accepting the truth that some pain is too great to bear alone, we invite Christ to sustain us along the way.

This world does not offer what we need to make it when the bottom falls out. Blame, anger, and busyness will not get you where you want to be . . . to the place of peace on this side of heaven. Embrace the truth that Christ made your child *just as she is* (Psalm 139). He alone is sovereign (Daniel 4:34b–35), and *His perfect love for you will cast out all fear* (1 John 4:18). God can do in you and through you what you cannot do for yourself (Romans 7:15–8:11). *He is good and is doing good things* despite the terrible circumstances you find yourself in (John 10:11; Romans 8:28). And He will, in the final analysis, *turn your sorrows into joy* (Matthew 5:4; 2 Thessalonians 2:16–17).

If you haven't already, surrender your burden to the almighty God. Once freed, you are ready to move into places of greater strength and peace.

Movement Two: From Grief to Hope

Once we identify our expectations, grief, and loss, we can come full circle. Before we can look with hope to the future, we must release what will never be. This work can be extremely lonely and painful, especially as our children undergo evaluations, goal-setting sessions, and medical assessments. Each time, some goals are met, others need more work, and some are written off as unattainable. When we face the fact that our children may never accomplish a certain goal or attain a particular desire, we feel a profound sense of loss and sorrow.

The grieving process involves anger and protest, denial and depression. Going through this process takes time and usually involves the assistance of a close friend and counselor. As you grieve, connecting with others is comforting. And grief is ultimately freeing.

When we do not allow ourselves to grieve, several things happen. First, we stop the growth process. When we hold hurt inside, it evolves into anger, depression, and internal conflict. This delays our ability to move forward because our coping

For Families of Children with Special Needs

resources are used up. Secondly, internal sorrow limits our availability to others . . . our mates, our other children, our friends, and so on. Lastly, when we choose to hold onto our sadness, we stop watching God do great things in and around us. When we grieve, a space is created within us for God to fill.

A cleansing process occurs when we grieve. Over the past five years, there have been several distinct times when I sat and wept for hours. My husband sat with me and held me as I cried. I was so sad that our son Jonathan would never be able to do things I wished he could do. But when I took time to grieve over what was lost, a vast resource of hope became available. From there, the future began to look much brighter.

Movement Three: From Isolation to Connection

When we first learned of our son Jonathan's PDD/NOS diagnosis, I wanted to shut out the world. But, in as many ways as possible, I identified my expectations and tried to face reality. I began the grief process, weeping over losses and trying to find new hopes for his little underdeveloped system.

But then we were informed that our other son, Austin, had language processing challenges and learning disabilities. My world caved in again. It was as if I said, "That's it!! I give up!" I wanted to shut out everybody and everything. I wanted to curl up in a corner and not ever move again. But I had a husband and children who needed a wife and mother. I had several friends who continued to encourage me and draw me out of my isolation. I had other women who sat on my floor and cried with me. Even some of Jonathan's specialists comforted me in my times of sorrow.

When the downside of the roller coaster invades our fragile world, it is easy to isolate, to shut down and go inward for a while. We may feel that no one has ever faced this before. We want to give up trying. We give up trying to see the bright side.

There are times when isolation is essential for gathering information and collecting our thoughts and resources for the tough road ahead. But isolation can also be destructive. When we lack connection to others, we begin to believe things that may not be true. We can become self-focused and then ill equipped to assist those who need us.

In contrast, when we connect with others, we find resources, strength, and hope. We gain courage to face what we could not face alone. Our relationships empower us to see possibilities and not just limitations. Connectedness to others also helps balance our perspective. In addition, connection to others is a comfort in grief. When our children struggle or fall short, our shared sorrow is half the sorrow. When our children overcome an obstacle, our shared joy is multiplied. I've learned that navigating life's storms becomes much easier when we set sail with fellow travelers.

Movement Four: Bondage to Strength

Many parents lament, "If I only had a diagnosis, I would feel better about everything." Or "I wish his problems had a label . . . I want to know exactly what I'm facing with him." Living with a disability brings an added amount of insecurity to life. Disabilities just don't fit into our little "life box." They force us to face the fact that we aren't in control of our circumstances. But beyond this realization, we have hope.

Joni Eareckson Tada lives as a quadriplegic. Her body is limited to a wheelchair and the assistance of others. But is that the limit of her abilities? For those who know her, the answer is no! She is an accomplished artist, musician, visionary, missionary, and giver of hope to millions around the world. She has seen past her limitations and her wheelchair to see who she is as a person, created in the image of her Creator, Jesus Christ.

So it is with every person on this earth. Created in the image of God, regardless of the label or limitations, each person has value and freedom. The child with Angleman syndrome, the autistic who has no language or is unable to engage in the outside world, the severely handicapped . . . all have the essence of God our Creator in them.

We must recognize the value of each person, no matter how this world labels him or her. I am not proposing that we live in fantasyland, thinking we will accomplish the impossible. I am proposing that we work within the parameters of what is true and find freedoms that exist within those boundaries. The movement from bondage to freedom and strength becomes filled with anticipation and joy. And we discover truths and see aspects of life that we never would have noticed if God had not brought this child with special needs into our home.

---

1. Barbara Gill, *Changed by A Child: Companion Notes for Parents of a Child with a Disability*, paperback ed. (New York, N.Y.: Broadway Books by arrangement with Doubleday, 2001), pp. 1, 202.
2. Judith Loseff Lavin, *Special Kids Need Special Parents: A Resource for Parents of Children with Special Needs* (New York, N.Y.: The Berkeley Publishing Group, Penguin Putnam Inc., 2001), p. 4.

For Families of Children with Special Needs

My Struggle . . . My Blessing?

by Suzanne Keffer
Writer, Creative Ministries, Insight for Living

As a child born with cerebral palsy (CP), I questioned God many times. Born nine weeks early, I weighed only three pounds and four ounces. My dad affectionately referred to my lowest weight of two pounds, twelve ounces as "just eight sticks of butter," and my mom dressed me in doll clothes for two months. However, it would be several years before they knew I had a problem.

The fact that I failed to walk until two-and-a-half signaled the first warning. The next alarm flashed when I walked only on my toes. I can still hear my mother's voice echoing, "Put your heels down." But no matter how hard I tried, I could not walk like the other kids. I longed to run the bases at recess, to flip off the diving board, or just to climb the stairs at school without losing my balance and falling down. Most of all, I begged God to let me walk flat-footed so that the other children would not make fun of me. God's Word said He loved me and promised to bless me, so I knew that He could cure my cerebral palsy. Surely, if God loved me, He would grant my prayer.

At night, I knelt at the side of my bed asking God once again to take away my CP. And in the morning, I climbed onto the bus feeling the cruel stares pierce through me another time. As a first-grader, I did not understand how my lack of oxygen at birth deserved Brad's insults at school. He performed his daily routine at lunch in the school cafeteria, walking high on his toes mimicking, "Look at me, I'm Suzanne." And everyone did look, including me. I wouldn't let them see my tears. I only showed those to my mother. In Psalm 56:8, the Lord reminded me that He kept my tears in His bottle. And I said, "I know, but why haven't you granted my prayer?"

Every day, my mom encouraged me to believe God's Word over Brad's taunts. Though she didn't quote Psalm 139, she often showed me that I was "fearfully and wonderfully made." I still remember the collection of brightly colored shoelaces she bought me when I had to wear a dreadful pair of black and white corrective shoes with steel-plated soles (which eventually snapped). My Dad never let me use my condition as an excuse. He expected me to do my best and saw beyond my limitations, exhorting me to develop the gifts God had given me. My older brother valued me, helping me onto the bus and scowling at Brad all the way to his seat.

As I grew physically, the Lord also matured me spiritually. Through my family and His Word, He abundantly proved Psalm 84:11, "No good thing does He withhold from those who walk uprightly" (NASB). He taught me how to deeply depend on Him and to value how He made me rather than how I walked. I learned at a young age to let my identity rest on Christ rather than on my abilities or disabilities. And Brad's ridicule gave me the gift of compassion, a treasure I might never have received without him.

In the sixth grade, God brought me another good thing. I had never heard of Texas Scottish Rite Hospital for Children, but they had heard of cerebral palsy. These volunteer doctors had perfected a procedure to lengthen Achilles tendons and hamstrings by partially severing them. Just as a nicked rubber band stretches to a longer length, my muscles would lengthen and rebuild themselves when they were cut.

At my pre-op appointment, the smell of fresh popcorn filled the waiting room as the spinning spokes of bicycles whirred above my head. Two prosthetic-wearing aviators pedaled a blimp furiously through the sky. I wondered if I had missed school to go to the hospital or the fair. Just then, a clown with shoes uglier than mine honked his horn at me, making me laugh. Children with metal-braced legs creaked stiffly toward the pink-haired clown to get a rainbow balloon. A five-year-old boy in a wheelchair clapped his hands in delight as the circus mime skipped toward him. Though I could not understand his slurred words, his smile said it all. A little girl with plaster legs rolled herself toward me.

"My name's Jenn. Do you want some popcorn?"

"Sure," I answered. "Do they hurt?"

"My legs? Sometimes, but this surgery hurt way less than the other four. I only have two more to go."

"The other four. Two more to go?" I thought, trying to hide my shock.

"How many do you have to have?" she asked.

"One."

"Wow, you're really lucky. You'll get to go back to regular school in no time."

When I returned to Sam Houston Elementary, I felt like a poster child with two full-length plaster casts and crutches. As I watched my friends play kickball, I wondered if Jenn was getting to play outside that day. My four-legged status certainly gave Brad more material for his daily routine. But when I remembered Jenn, his words didn't sting as much as they had before.

On my last post-op visit to the popcorn fair nearly two months later, the metal saw reminded me of a supersonic pizza cutter as it smoked its way through my plaster legs. The powder haze irritated my eyes. The air smelled electrical—the way it did the first time Dad turned on the heat each winter. I had grown to depend on those plaster shells that lay lifeless on the floor. My own legs felt frail without their plaster shields. Still propped on the crutches, I feebly took my first new steps. "Left crutch, right leg, right crutch, left leg."

As the weeks passed, I mastered bipedal walking again. But this time, I "heel walked" rather than "toe walked." Twenty years later, I still walk with an irregular gait. Now I have a hard time even standing on my toes. With my lack of balance and coordination, I would flunk a sobriety test sober. However, I consider myself fortunate to have had cerebral palsy.

In his sovereignty, God used a birth defect to bless me. Through cerebral palsy, He taught me dependence upon Him, identity in Him, and compassion through Him. Most importantly, He used my CP to show me how to think of others rather than focus on myself. I thank my Father often that in His grace, He allowed me to be a "toe walker" for the first 12 years of my life. I also thank Him that He never took away my weakness completely because the day-to-day dealing with it drives me to rely on Him. My gratitude flows from my certainty of God's promise, "No good thing will He withhold from those who walk uprightly" (Ps. 84:11 NASB).

Your Child . . . Your Calling?

If God has given you a child with special needs, you may find yourself asking why or praying for a miraculous cure. If the answers you desire don't come and the challenges of caring for your son or daughter continue, remember that the God of the universe has entrusted you with the amazing task of embracing a child that many people would reject. While it's not the baseball games or ballet recitals that you imagined, it is a divine invitation to nurture a "fearfully and wonderfully made" being. She may never hear your voice or say your name. He may thrash every time you hold him. She may have a four-year-old mind in a twenty-four-year-old body. They are God's creations. You are the steward He chose to care for the precious soul inside an imperfect body.

No matter the degree of your child's disability, treat him or her with **CARE**:

- *Challenge him or her to excel.* Whether your child faces minor challenges or major obstacles, always stimulate his or her development. While distinguishing between red and blue or drinking through a straw may seem like a small victory to you, the confidence your child will gain is immeasurable. Even if he or she never masters a task, the time spent with you and others will benefit him or her.

- *Affirm his or her value.* Like all children, kids with special needs yearn to know their worth. When your child interacts with people like Brad who don't understand her condition, she may question her value. Be prepared to talk frankly about her developmental differences. Teach him to tell others about it when they ask. Comfort him when he hurts. Remind her that God made her. Offer him the opportunity to learn forgiveness as he faces others' jeers.

- *Realize his or her limitations without limiting his or her potential.* While you may need to assist your child in many areas, don't allow your help to become a hindrance to his or her independence. Guide him with as much freedom as possible. By empowering your child to do some things on her own, you give her self-assurance. If you think he might fail, let him try. If it takes her a little longer to dress herself, get up earlier. If her clothes don't match, don't worry about it.

For Families of Children with Special Needs

- *Encourage him or her to interact with peers and people in the community.* Don't isolate your child from others in an effort to protect him or her. She needs to socialize, and you need outside support. Let her get to know other children—both kids with typical development and kids with special needs. Ask older kids or adult friends you trust to spend time with him. He should learn to relate to people outside his family. Cultivate an environment that will allow your child to bloom socially. When he stutters, someone may snicker. When she asks for help up the stairs, the first person may say "No." But the next "Yes" could be the new friend she never would have met if it weren't for the first "No." When your child's skills do not allow him to function on his own, consider assisted care. As he matures, a special needs daycare can provide a social outlet. If she wants to live in a group home at eighteen, don't hold her back.

If you **CARE** for your child well, your son or daughter will likely look beyond his or her needs to see the special kid you see. Her "Reasons I'm Special List" will include her Maker, family, friends, abilities, and challenges.

Though your ideal family photograph probably didn't include a child with special needs, God's perfect portrait did. Just because your picture has changed, don't forget that God has given you a good thing. Desire the best for this soul that He placed in your life. You may never watch him hit a homer or see her dance Swan Lake, but you can focus on realizing new dreams with the extraordinary kid God has entrusted to you.

Something to Shout About!
Family Life and Children with Special Needs

An Interview with Vivian Shudde, Director of Brookwood Community

by Bryce Klabunde
Vice President, Pastoral Ministries, Insight for Living

Vivian Shudde understands the heartaches and joys of family life with children with special needs. She has experienced them firsthand. She grew up with a younger sister who had severe handicaps, and she has reared her own mentally challenged son. Her degrees in special education and her position as director of Brookwood Community, a non-profit residential work facility for adults with functional disabilities, give her credibility to speak on disabilities. But she will tell you that her highest qualification to talk about parenting children with special needs is that she is a parent herself. In this article based on our conversation with her, Vivian shares her insights about accepting reality, surviving marital stress, and helping siblings deal with their feelings. Most importantly, she shares her positive spirit, which is an inspiration to anyone who has a family member with special needs.

Q: **What first touched your heart to reach out to people with special needs?**

A: My sister. My younger sister Vicki was a one-year-old when she got sick— mumps contracted in the church nursery. Then a complication followed that turned into meningitis, causing severe brain damage. She was not expected to live. The disease left her unable to function. The doctors told my parents, "You need to put her into an institution, or she will ruin your family." That was forty-seven years ago, and back then, that's what most people did.

I was two years old at the time, and Vicki was one. I have another sister, Vita, who was three years old. So we were three, two, and one. In most books, that's enough to put anyone under!

Q: **How did your mother respond to your sister's condition?**

A: My mom was going to cure Vicki. Vicki got sick in an instant; she could get well in an instant. Every single technique in the United States was used to help my sister. People say, "I can cure your child if you just do this program or that program." There is so much out there that could absorb every bit of financial resources that you have.

A parent wants to go where someone will say, "This program or this auditory training or this *whatever* will cure your child." If one doctor says, "I can cure you," and another doctor says, "I can just help you reach your potential," you're going to go with the person who says, "I can cure you." The reality, however, is that the best that most can hope for is that the child will reach his or her potential.

Q: **So Vicki's presence in your family had a positive influence in your childhood.**

A: The whole family was involved in the fun ways of helping Vicki with motor development and so forth. We had an obstacle course in our back yard. We had a trampoline. We had lots of neat things that were because of Vicki.

Q: **Never did you imagine that your first baby would be born with special needs, too.**

A: When I was pregnant with our first child, Wilson, we socially adopted a forty-year-old individual with Down syndrome. I thought it would be a great opportunity for my child to have a disabled person in our home. When Wilson was born, he wasn't going to have any of these problems. He was going to be a Harvard grad! Aren't all first-born kids Harvard grads?

Q: **What emotions did you experience when you found out that your son was mentally challenged?**

A: Disbelief. When you're pregnant, you worry. I worried about cleft pallet. I worried about a physical handicap of some nature. Mental retardation does not run in our family. Vicki got sick at age one. It didn't dawn on me that I would have a child who was mentally challenged.

Q: **How do you explain to your son what is "wrong" with him?**

A: We don't use the word *wrong*. In our home, we tell our son that he's handicapped. The way that you tell your son that he's handicapped is first establishing what is *handicapped*. One person wears eyeglasses, another person doesn't. He wears contacts, she doesn't. We're all handicapped in one way or another. If my job depended on me singing, I'd be in a state institution! We're all handicapped. That perspective helps him understand.

Q: **How do parents accept their disabled child's condition?**

A: It is a grieving process. When Wilson was age two months, my mom started saying, "I think Wilson is delayed." I was furious. "What do you mean? You're just looking for stuff. Mother, you deal with it day in and day out. There's nothing wrong with him."

When the pediatrician saw Wilson at two months, he said, "I don't think there's anything wrong." *So there.*

Well, then at four and five months, he was not rolling over. He was not picking up toys. You begin that developmental fear. You know those books that say at three months, babies are supposed to do this; at four months, they're supposed to do that; at five months, and so on. I might as well have been at a funeral home reading those books, because my child never made his benchmarks.

For Families of Children with Special Needs

Q: **The grieving process can be very difficult. What are some of the most painful times?**

A: Your child's birthdays and other children's birthday parties can be very painful. You may have been pregnant at the same time as a friend. You had your baby showers together. Now, all of a sudden, you're not on the team. Your kid's sitting in the corner at the party, drooling. Children with special needs may be invited to the party. But they're never a real part of it.

Q: **Parents tend to isolate themselves and their special-needs children, don't they?**

A: Moms with special-needs children are uneasy about their own child's development, and they're living in such fear that they create walls and barriers between themselves and their past relationships with other mothers. It's too painful to want to go to McDonald's with other five-year-olds, because it's in your face. Their children are playing on the playground; your child is playing with a french fry. You have to go through a grieving process—the loss of the child that you thought you were owed.

Q: **Part of the grieving process is denial and anger, bargaining and depression. Did you experience any of those?**

A: I am never critical of a parent of a special-needs child who is in denial. I'm a developmental specialist. Who should know more than Vivian Shudde about the reality of disabilities? I majored in it. Had a sister with it. But I put my disabled child in the *regular* mothers' day out program! Because if I put him in there, then, when someone asked, "Where's Wilson going to school?" I didn't want to say, "The school for children with special needs." I did go through denial.

What helped was getting tired of living on the roller coaster. Any positive comment by someone meant that Wilson might be OK, but any negative comment meant, "Oh no, he *is* mentally retarded." You're on this constant roller coaster, and I decided, "No more." I had to accept reality concerning Wilson.

Q: **Having a child with special needs puts enormous strain on a marriage. What are some of the unique stresses?**

A: It certainly creates stress. There is *always* the need for a babysitter. Just last weekend, for example, I was trying to find a babysitter for Wilson, who is 19 years old now. Where do you find babysitters for your 19-year-old mentally handicapped son? Special-needs children grow up, and now you have a functionally disabled adult to care for.

There is no free time. There is no down time. Sometimes it's difficult to hear parents who talk about being up with their sick child for three nights. And you're thinking, "I haven't slept through the night in *years!*" There is no sleeping late. Your life is not your own, and there is no hope for having your own life.

For Families of Children with Special Needs

Q: **What have you and your husband done to cope with these stresses?**

A: We have always been huge proponents of counseling. I don't know how marriages survive without counseling. Another source of help for us has been our parents. A lot of grandparents cannot accept a special-needs child. They just think the child is going to outgrow it; he's just a late bloomer. My grandparents kept my sister, Vicki, one night of every weekend. And now my parents keep my son one night of every weekend. You have to make that time to go out or to have peace in the home or to just do your own thing.

Some moms will not allow even the husband to keep the child, because sometimes the child is in such strenuous programs that the mother feels that if she's not there, the kid will not survive. They're over focused on the child, and it's really tough on the marriage.

Q: **What about siblings? How can parents encourage healthy relationships between siblings of children with special needs?**

A: We had a lot of activity in our home because we were on a very stringent motor development program with Vicki. But I was never forced, nor was my other sister, to do anything with Vicki. It was simply on an If-you'd-like-to basis.

Some mothers try to over involve their special-needs child with their brother or sister. A mother, for example, may take her autistic child to his brother's basketball games. The autistic child loves the games because of the lights and the activity, and he can run around—but what about the brother?

Now will the brother say, "Don't bring my brother to the basketball game because he embarrasses me?" No way. Siblings of handicapped kids are incredibly empathetic. They would never hurt their handicapped sibling's feelings.

As the parent, you have to take the initiative. Don't say to the brother, "We're going to leave Johnny at home because he might embarrass you at the basketball game." That would make the brother feel guilty. Instead, arrange a babysitter or family member to take the special-needs child on an outing to get ice cream or something. Then say to the brother, "You have a basketball game today and Johnny has been invited for a special day, too." Find a way to make the brother feel OK about having his time at the basketball game.

Q: **What are some other ways to help siblings handle their feelings toward their handicapped brother or sister?**

A: Don't push one sibling on the other. You don't want to "buy" their love for the handicapped brother or sister by promising them something, but you do want to help build the bond between them. For example, my handicapped sister, Vicki, didn't have much to offer my "normal" daughter, Sarah, when she was younger. However, whatever gift my daughter wanted the most for Christmas, such as this particular pink wallet, that pink wallet came from Aunt Vicki. My daughter always wanted a cat. Guess who gave her a cat? Aunt Vicki. In my daughter's mind, Aunt Vicki was a treasured person in our home. Children grow to love handicapped family members for who they are in their world.

Here's another example. Our daughter really wanted a trampoline. But we got the trampoline because Wilson needed it for developmental reasons. We told our daughter, "Aren't you fortunate to have a brother like Wilson?" Our daughter has a handicapped brother, so we get to go to the front of the lines at Disney World! We have a three-wheeled tricycle! Think of those items in your home that are treasured, and tie them to the handicapped person. In that way, the sibling gets to brag that he or she has a handicapped brother or sister.

Q: **So instead of a liability, the handicapped brother or sister becomes an asset in the mind of the siblings.**

A: Yes! Having a family member with a handicap is something to shout about! And that attitude starts with the mom's heart. If I'm uneasy with the child—which I was for five years, so I can identify with 99 percent of parents—then that attitude pervades the family.

A positive attitude about a difficult situation doesn't just happen. How did you gain this attitude?

After praying for healing and expecting a miracle in the life of our family, God answered that prayer . . . in me! He answered it by showing me that nowhere in the Bible does it state that a certain IQ or a behavior is "normal." Where in Scripture does it state the plumb line for what is normal? It's not there. What God has given you is *normal*.

A person may have a body that is handicapped or a mind that does not function like everyone else's. In the eyes of the world, they are not normal, but how does God see that person? Wilson probably has a closer spiritual relationship with the Lord than anyone I know. Spiritually, he *is* a Harvard grad! Isn't that the most important thing? We pray for people with special needs like Wilson to get healed. But God says, "Healed from what?"

Q: **Any final advice?**

A: Be creative. Get a sense of humor! We have such funny stories at our house. We had Communion at church, and they were passing the grape juice, and my son looked up and said, "Do y'all have Diet Coke here?" They're laughing. We're laughing. One time for Halloween, my son wanted to be the preacher of our church. So he dressed up like our pastor, and he took the collection plate from door to door. We gave him tracts to hand out. The great news is that no one will turn down anything from a handicapped kid. If he passes out a tract, and if he asks people if they're saved, he can get by with it. The Lord gives them an opportunity and boldness to minister with no repercussions.

For Families of Children with Special Needs

There's a whole other side to having a child with special needs. It's the joy! This perspective can only be painted from God's point of view. He's laughing too—only at us—trying to cure these people who, in His eyes, are already healed!

Compassion in Action
The Benefits of Special Needs Ministry

by Cliff Ritter
Pastor, Pastoral Ministries, Insight for Living

As the disciples jockeyed among themselves for status in the kingdom, Jesus stood a child by His side and said, "Whoever welcomes this little child in my name welcomes me; and whoever welcomes me welcomes the one who sent me. For he who is least among you all—he is the greatest" (Luke 9:48 NIV).

Welcoming children with special needs into the life of the church is like welcoming one of the least among us all—indeed, they are the greatest. To welcome these children into our lives is to welcome the Lord, so close are they to His heart. However, many churches find it difficult to launch programs to help families with children with special needs. High-profile ministries command the lion's share of attention from pastors and church boards. Why should a church invest its resources to minister to this small group of families? What benefit will this ministry to a few bring to the many?

Special Needs Ministries Benefit the Extended Family

The benefits of a Special Needs Ministry extend far beyond a single child, challenged by physical, emotional, or mental disabilities. Parents, siblings, and a whole network of family members also find a place of refuge when the church remains open to their needs. Given a respite from the burden of constant caregiving, families can take advantage of the resources offered by the church by attending Sunday school, worshiping in the sanctuary, seeking support and counseling, or participating in the life of the church in other ways.

Special Needs Ministries Provide Opportunities for Service

Christ demonstrated His service to others and His love for us by offering Himself on the Cross. He served those who followed him by humbling Himself before them, washing their feet in one final gesture of servant leadership. In that moment, Jesus said, "Now that I, your Lord and Teacher, have washed your feet, you also should wash one another's feet" (John 13:14 NIV). His commitment to serving others extended even to the one who would later betray him for a few silver coins.

Special Needs Ministry provides a multitude of opportunities to wash another's feet as Jesus did. Pushing a wheel chair, reading a Bible story, helping to choose an appropriate color, or simply holding a fearful hand are ways we can put our servant's towel into action in loving service to children with special needs. Success is measured in delightful laughter, a simple smile, or tears that vanish before mommy returns. The most important qualification is our presence and a

For the Church

willingness to serve. The payoff comes when we recognize the Lord in the face of a beloved child.

The Apostle Paul implores us to ". . . serve one another in love" (Galatians 5:13 NIV). He writes, "Be devoted to one another in brotherly love. Honor one another above yourselves" (Romans 12:10 NIV). The honorable work of serving one another in love generates a deeper understanding of God's devotion to his people. Sacrificial service is the catalyst for growing spiritually robust followers of Christ.

A Special Needs Ministry offers an environment where genuine needs can be met with heartfelt compassion. Church members and volunteers quickly come to understand what it means to be devoted to one another. Honoring others above ourselves helps us to forge a path to the foot of the Cross, where we too are blessed, honored, and served.

Special Needs Ministries Deepen Character

The Apostle Paul instructs the church to "be completely humble and gentle; be patient, bearing with one another in love" (Ephesians 4:2 NIV). A ministry to children with special needs emphasizes these essential character traits. Humility, gentleness, and patience serve as cornerstones in the life of the church. Bearing with one another in love, the community of faith grows more Christ-like through acts of charity and kindness to one another. A Special Needs Ministry commits itself to meeting the needs of every family in the church, specifically focusing on those with the unique challenge presented by a child with special needs.

Special Needs Ministries Help Church Members Model Christ

As the church matures in its commitment to serving "the least of those among us," we are reminded of Christ's affirmation, ". . . whatever you did for one of the least of these brothers of mine, you did for me" (Matthew 25:40 NIV). The Apostle Paul exhorts fellow believers to "submit to one another out of reverence for Christ" (Ephesians 5:21 NIV). Growing closer to Christ is the ultimate motivation for serving others in His name. Through our commitment to serve others, we model the example set forth by Christ. Lasting friendships, nurtured in the context of a helping relationship, strengthen the bonds of Christian love. We grow in Christ, and in relationship with one another, as we follow His example of servant leadership. As we share one another's burdens, we gain a holy perspective on serving others.

Conclusion

A ministry to families with special needs children holds the promise of changing the community. How often have our churches pondered taking the Gospel to distant mission fields, hoping to help others with more "significant" ministry concerns, while overlooking families in the local community with genuine needs? Community awareness draws attention to unfulfilled needs in our own backyards.

Ministering to families with special needs children is an undiscovered mission field for many churches.

Children with special needs play a vital role in the church. They teach us, by example, about compassion, commitment, and unconditional love. Families striving to meet the daily challenge of caring for a child with special needs cherish the opportunity to participate in the life of the church. Churches are uniquely positioned to meet the needs of these families. Never before has our calling been so clearly established, or so urgently needed. Welcoming families and children with special needs demonstrates our commitment to the whole body of Christ, from the greatest to the least.

Shepherding the Little Lambs

Pastoral Care to Families of Children with Special Needs

by Graham Lyons
Pastor, Pastoral Ministries, Insight for Living

> "What man among you, if he has a hundred sheep and has lost one of them, does not leave the ninety-nine in the open pasture and go after the one which is lost until he finds it?" (Luke 15:4 NASB)

Jesus' parable of the shepherd who leaves his flock to look for one lost sheep portrays the heart of the Father and paints a warm picture of pastoral care.

As pastors and church leaders caring for the flock today, we can easily forget the little sheep that are small, out of sight, and seemingly insignificant. The members of a church look to the pastor for cues of how to show compassion. They long to see examples of pastoral care. One of the clearest messages that we can send about caring is to touch the life of a child with special needs.

King David was a shepherd as a boy, and his shepherd's heart characterized his life and reign. It was displayed when David invited Mephibosheth, Jonathan's crippled son, to join him at his royal table (2 Samuel 9). Just as David shared his meals with Mephibosheth, we can share the bounty of God's spiritual banquet with those who have special needs. They may not find much care in our culture; however, they should find care in God's flock.

Children with special needs and their families provide both an opportunity for godly ministry and a way to set an example of caring to church members. Here are a few ways that you can reach out to them as their shepherd:

- *Give time and touch.* One simple way to minister is to give time and touch to such a child on Sunday morning. A simple prayer for the child while touching him or her will demonstrate love to the child and encourage the parents. They need to know that they and their child with special needs matter to the pastor.

- *Visit the families of children with special needs.* Another possibility for ministry is to periodically visit the parents and the child. Since they often may need special medical attention, make certain to meet them at the hospital for prayer and encouragement.

- *Provide practical assistance.* Ask the parents about practical ways the church can help. Since the parents may be overwhelmed by the time and effort needed for routine care, perhaps you can arrange for child care and give the parents tickets for a night at the theatre and dinner. Such a simple gesture may just be the act that encourages them to continue on. Ask them how you can minister to them or their child. Let them see your shepherd's heart.

For the Church

- *Give special attention on Sundays.* Another way to minister is to periodically visit the special needs class on Sunday. Interact with the children and encourage the class workers. When it's possible you may want to consider taking the family and their child to lunch.

When you organize a special needs ministry, your personal involvement and time will help solidify its importance and encourage those who invest their time in this ministry. It will give a visible example of the Father's love for these little sheep.

What Does God Say?

A Biblical Perspective of Children with Special Needs

by Kelly Arabie
Women's Ministry Associate, Pastoral Ministries, Insight for Living

Down syndrome. Cerebral palsy. Spina bifida. The names sound so clinical and cold. With each genetic disorder or disease, however, is the face of a child. The world says that these children are less than "normal." But what does God say about these precious ones? What perspective does His Word give us toward people with disabilities?

Here is a topical list of verses that share God's heart toward those with special needs.

We Are Made in the Image of God

So God created man in his own image, in the image of God he created him; male and female he created them. (Genesis 1:27 NIV)

For in the image of God He made man. (Genesis 9:6b NASB)

With the tongue we praise our Lord and Father, and with it we curse men, who have been made in God's likeness. (James 3:9 NIV)

God Weaves Together Our Bodies and Our Lives According to His Sovereign Plan

For you created my inmost being;
   you knit me together in my mother's womb.

I praise you because I am fearfully and wonderfully made;
   your works are wonderful,
   I know that full well.

My frame was not hidden from you
   when I was made in the secret place.

When I was woven together in the depths of the earth,
   your eyes saw my unformed body.

All the days ordained for me
   were written in your book
   before one of them came to be. (Psalm 139:13–16 NIV)

Then Job replied to the Lord:

"I know that you can do all things;
   no plan of yours can be thwarted. . . .

My ears had heard of you
   but now my eyes have seen you." (Job 42:1–2, 5 NIV)

Theological and Biblical Perspectives

We can hold fast to the assurance that a special-needs child is not a mistake. But there are still days when we hurt and grieve the frustration and the turmoil that naturally come in day-to-day living. What does God say about our pain?

He Gives Us Comfort

But those who suffer he delivers in their suffering; he speaks to them in their affliction. (Job 36:15 NIV)

But you are a shield around me, O Lord;
  you bestow glory on me and lift up my head.
To the Lord I cry aloud,
  and he answers me from his holy hill.
I lie down and sleep;
  I wake again, because the Lord sustains me. (Psalm 3:3–5 NIV)

The Lord is a refuge for the oppressed,
  a stronghold in times of trouble.
Those who know your name will trust in you,
  for you, Lord, have never forsaken those who seek you.
  (Psalm 9:9–10 NIV)

And my God will supply all your needs according to His riches in glory in Christ Jesus. (Philippians 4:19 NASB)

He Gives Us Each Other

But now God has placed the members, each one of them, in the body, just as He desired. . . . And if one member suffers, all the members suffer with it; if one member is honored, all the members rejoice with it. (1 Corinthians 12:18, 26 NASB)

"A new command I give you: Love one another. As I have loved you, so you must love one another. By this all men will know that you are my disciples, if you love one another." (John 13:34–35 NIV)

Therefore encourage one another and build each other up, just as in fact you are doing. (1 Thessalonians 5:11 NIV)

And let us consider how we may spur one another on toward love and good deeds. Let us not give up meeting together, as some are in the habit of doing, but let us encourage one another—and all the more as you see the Day approaching. (Hebrews 10:24–25 NIV)

Now that you have purified yourselves by obeying the truth so that you have sincere love for your brothers, love one another deeply, from the heart. (1 Peter 1:22 NIV)

He Reminds Us That Our Present Circumstance Is Not the End

> And we, who with unveiled faces all reflect the Lord's glory, are being transformed into his likeness with ever-increasing glory, which comes from the Lord, who is the Spirit. (2 Corinthians 3:18 NIV)

> In this you greatly rejoice, though now for a little while you may have had to suffer grief in all kinds of trials. These have come so that your faith—of greater worth than gold, which perishes even though refined by fire—may be proved genuine and may result in praise, glory and honor when Jesus Christ is revealed. (1 Peter 1:6–7 NIV)

A special-needs child requires sacrificial giving of oneself. But Jesus said, "Whatever you did for one of the least of these brothers of mine, you did for me" (Matthew 25:40 NIV).

What Can Our Response Be?

> Search me, O God, and know my heart;
>   test me and know my anxious thoughts.
> See if there is any offensive way in me,
>   and lead me in the way everlasting. (Psalm 139:23–24 NIV)

> Vindicate the weak and fatherless;
>   Do justice to the afflicted and destitute.
> Rescue the weak and needy;
>   Deliver them out of the hand of the wicked. (Psalm 82:3–4 NASB)

> You also, as living stones, are being built up as a spiritual house for a holy priesthood, to offer up spiritual sacrifices acceptable to God through Jesus Christ. (1 Peter 2:5 NASB)

> Through Him then, let us continually offer up a sacrifice of praise to God, that is, the fruit of lips that give thanks to His name. And do not neglect doing good and sharing, for with such sacrifices God is pleased. (Hebrews 13:15–16 NASB)

> Therefore I urge you, brethren, by the mercies of God, to present your bodies a living and holy sacrifice, acceptable to God, which is your spiritual service of worship. (Romans 12:1 NASB)

As you continue to minister to a special-needs child in your sphere of influence, listen to God's voice and remember Paul's exhortation to the Galatians and to us: "Let us not lose heart in doing good, for in due time we will reap if we do not grow weary" (Galatians 6:9 NASB).

The Dignity of Humanity and the Sanctity of Life

by Robert A. Pyne, Th.D.
Professor of Systematic Theology, Dallas Theological Seminary

After centuries of wrestling with the problem of human suffering, western society has largely agreed upon an answer, placing its trust in technology. Technology ultimately represents a false hope, for it cannot keep its promises, but we find ourselves increasingly enamored with the possibilities. If there is sickness, it can be cured; if there is pain, it can be relieved; if there is disease, it can be eradicated; if there are birth defects, they can be prevented. All of this is possible, we tell ourselves, if we grow in knowledge and in technological proficiency. But if those things ultimately fail us and suffering becomes unbearable, we may consider one last option: life can be gently terminated.

Most Christians rightly respond to that possibility (and certain technological procedures like embryonic stem-cell research) by appealing to the sanctity of human life. Unfortunately, the idea that people have unique, inherent dignity regardless of their capacities is not widely embraced. For example, Helga Kuhse, who directs a center for bioethics in Australia, asked whether the sanctity of human life could really be defended. "Here we should note that I shall not, when speaking of the sanctity-of-life doctrine, be using the term 'sanctity' in a specifically religious sense. While the doctrine may well have its source in theology, I am not concerned with the question of whether or not the doctrine is true to some theological tradition or other, but rather with the question of whether it can be defended on non-theological grounds." In other words, can one argue that all human beings have inherent dignity and unique value without appealing to some sort of divine authority?

I would suggest that from a biblical perspective, one cannot. People are unique not because they think differently than chimpanzees (though they probably do), and human lives are valuable not because they contribute to a better world (though they probably do that, too). People have inherent dignity and unique value because they have all been made in the image of God. Since every person has been created according to the divine image, every human life becomes sacred. Just as David would not lay a hand on Saul as God's anointed (1 Sam. 24:10), so we should not murder (or even curse) those who have been made in the image of God (Gen. 9:6; James 3:9–10).

This becomes a very important point in bioethical discussions like those taking place between Kuhse and her peers. If one assumes a naturalistic philosophy, which regards humanity as unique only in the sense that we have reached a higher stage

Theological and Biblical Perspectives

of evolutionary development, those who are less capable may easily be regarded as less valuable. On the other hand, if one believes that human dignity comes from God, one who seeks to honor God will honor those whom He has made in His image. The difference is especially apparent when considering those whom our society views as least valuable: the poor, the terminally ill, the elderly, the unborn, and the handicapped (Ps. 82:3–4; Prov. 14:31). Kuhse concluded that it would be right to kill patients painlessly, including handicapped infants, if their lives were not judged by others to be pleasant ones. This is not unlike a Newsweek essay, in which a woman argued that a severely handicapped man, Henry, should be put to sleep in the same manner as her suffering cat. In response to that article, I found myself in rare agreement with Derek Humphry of the Hemlock Society, who said that "to kill Henry, even out of mercy, would be murder in the worst degree."

I should probably add that my feelings on this issue are colored not only by my theology, but also by my experience. Our oldest son, Steve, had open-heart surgery when he was just eight months old. Unfortunately, some countries, doctors, and even some parents would not have allowed him to have that operation, even though it was necessary to save his life. Steve has Down syndrome, and too many people think that lives like his are not worth saving.

My temptation as a proud dad has always been to talk about the things that Steve enjoys doing, how quickly he learned to read, or how sincerely he loves the Lord, to try to convince others that his very happy life was worth saving. On the other hand, my job as a theologian is to say simply this: His life was worth saving because he has inherent dignity as a human being in the image of God. The same is true of little boys who never will learn to read and those whose lives don't look happy at all.

The treatment of the handicapped raises another important implication of the approach taken here toward the image of God. If the image of God consists simply of our rational, emotional, and volitional capacities, then certain severely handicapped persons (like anencephalic infants, for example) evidently lack God's image and may be judged less than human. People who lose those capabilities would lose something of their humanity, perhaps forfeiting inherent human rights. By contrast, I have argued that even our bodies have been formed in God's image as they have been made to reflect His glory. Since all persons still have the potential to be fully conformed to Christ's likeness and to act as vice-regents over creation, either in this life or the next, all human life is valuable.

In the West dehumanizing technologies and a disproportionate emphasis on comfortable lifestyles continually challenge this basic affirmation of life. Elsewhere the obstacles are different, but the essential issues remain the same. Twice I have taken trips to India, where so many people crowd the streets of cities, that human life is too easily regarded as of little value. Cattle and cobras are often worshiped as gods, while many of God's vice-regents live in desperate poverty. When so many have "exchanged the glory of the incorruptible God for an image in the form of corruptible man and of birds and four-footed animals and crawling creatures" (Rom. 1:23 NASB), the results are devastating.

Whether in India or America, the basic problem remains the same, as does the basic solution. Sin has prevented our world and the people in it from fulfilling the Genesis ideal, but if anyone is in Christ, there is a new creation. Glory is restored to the common, dignity to the dishonored, and dominion to the oppressed, but only through the gospel of Christ, who is the image of God.

Adapted from *Humanity and Sin: The Creation, Fall, and Redemption of Humanity*, Swindoll Leadership Library, Charles R. Swindoll, gen. ed. (Nashville, Tenn.: Word Publishing, 1999), pp. 68–70.

Notes

Notes

Notes

Notes

Notes

Notes